Teaching Comparative Law: Experiences and Reflections

Teaching Comparative Law: Experiences and Reflections

Katharina Boele-Woelki

eleven

Published, sold and distributed by Eleven
P.O. Box 85576
2508 CG The Hague
The Netherlands
Tel.: +31 70 33 070 33
Fax: +31 70 33 070 30
e-mail: sales@elevenpub.nl
www.elevenpub.com

Sold and distributed in USA and Canada
Independent Publishers Group
814 N. Franklin Street
Chicago, IL 60610, USA
Order Placement: +1 800 888 4741
Fax: +1 312 337 5985
orders@ipgbook.com
www.ipgbook.com

Eleven is an imprint of Boom (Den Haag).

ISBN 978-90-4730-194-3
ISBN 978-94-0011-372-5 (E-book)

© 2024 Katharina Boele-Woelki | Eleven

TABLE OF CONTENTS

PREFACE

"Comparative law being merely a method of study has no fixed content and there is no such thing as the 'standard' or even the 'optimum' comparative law course."
G. Winterton, 'Comparative Law Teaching', American Journal of Comparative Law, Vol. 23, No. 1, 1975, p. 118.

It was a great honour for me to deliver the 2022 Maastricht Private Law Lecture. I spoke about my experiences and reflections on teaching comparative law. I have been teaching comparative law for more than a quarter of a century, in different settings, at different times, in different places. No two lectures or workshops are the same. I think that it is fair to say that each course has had its own focus and served its own content. Of course, there are commonalities, principles, views, perspectives and methodological considerations that are always conveyed, but even a methodological foundation needs to be constantly updated. And neither does it stop there. The choice and sequence of topics is not prescribed, and the way in which students are involved and motivated should be subject to a constant review. This already requires our scientific curiosity and integrity. When I arrived at Bucerius Law School in Hamburg in 2015 after 20 years of teaching at the University of Utrecht, my approach to teaching comparative law changed fundamentally, as I taught both international students from all over the world and German students, fortunately in two different courses. Having never taught in my mother tongue before, only in Dutch and English, I have to admit that I had a number of difficulties in teaching in German at the beginning, as I was not familiar with the legal terminology. However, the new environment provided me with an excellent opportunity to reorientate and reorganise myself and to take advantage of the benefits offered by both groups. I will report on my experiences.[1]

Katharina Boele-Woelki

---

1   Several parts of this contribution are derived from: K. Boele-Woelki, 'Experiential Teaching of Comparative Law', *in* Boele-Woelki *et al.* (Eds.), *Festschrift für Karsten Schmidt*, C.H. Beck Verlag, 2019, pp. 133-141. They have been updated and extended.

1   The Subject of Comparative Law Teaching

As lawyers we have been trained in doubting ready-made solutions, questioning their rationale, and offering new solutions that are adapted to the changed circumstances. But how can we offer other solutions? The easiest way to find inspiration for developing a different solution or rule is to cross legal borders, since outside our own jurisdiction a plethora of different approaches and solutions exist which might provide a better approach, might be more efficient, might comply with our needs, and might, however, also dispel possible doubts that our solution is the right one under the given circumstances. In order to effectively use the many opportunities offered by looking across the border, training in comparative law is needed.

Teaching comparative law encompasses various components.[2] First, one can think of the history and use of comparative law. This can be deployed by telling the story of ancient Greek and Roman law[3] followed by classifications of jurisdictions into legal cultures[4] and legal families.[5] Legal transplants[6] and the global and regional unification and harmonization of the law through supranational organizations[7] are other areas where the use of comparative law can be clearly illustrated. Another approach consists of introductions to legal systems other than the one in which the students are educated. In Europe, usually the common law (the US and UK) and the civil law (France and

---

2   See K. Boele-Woelki & D.P. Fernández Arroyo & A. Senegacnik (Eds.), *Contemporary Challenges to the Teaching of Comparative Law, Ceremony of 16 May 2022 in Honour of 5 Great Comparatists*, Brussels, Larcier Intersentia, 2023.

3   See W. Hug, 'The History of Comparative Law', *Harvard Law Review*, Vol. 45 No. 6, Apr. 1932, pp. 1027-1070; G. Frankenberg, 'Critical Histories of Comparative Law', *in* M. D. Dubber & C. Tomlins (Eds.), *The Oxford Handbook of Legal History*, Oxford University Press, 2018, pp. 42-63.

4   See S. Koch & J. Øyrehagen Sunde (Eds.), *Comparing Legal Cultures*, Fagbokforlaget, 2020, with introductions to the Norwegian, Finnish, Estonian, German, Polish, England & Wales, Scottish, Belgian, French, Autrian, Italian, Romanian, American, Australian and Chinese Legal Cultures.

5   See U. Mattei, 'Three Patterns of Law', *American Journal of Comparative Law*, Vol. 45, No. 1, 1997, p. 44; Y. Chang & N. Garoupa & M. T. Wells, 'Drawing the Legal Family Tree: An Empirical Comparative Study of 108 Property Doctrines in 128 Jurisdictions', *Journal of Legal Analysis*, Vol. 13, No. 1, 2021, pp. 231-282; V. V. Palmer, 'A Descriptive and Comparative Overview', *in* V. V. Palmer (Ed.), *Mixed Jurisdictions Worldwide: The Third Legal Family*, 2nd ed., Cambridge University Press, 2012, pp. 19-91.

6   See R. Michaels, 'One Size Can Fit All, On the Mass Production of Legal Transplants', *in* G. Frankenberg (Ed.), *Order from Transfer–Studies in Comparative (Constitutional) Law*, Edward Elgar, 2013, available at https://ssrn.com/abstract=2191543 (retrieved on 30 June 2023).

7   See K. Boele-Woelki, 'Unifying and harmonizing substantive law and the role of conflict of laws', *Recueil des cours*, Vol. 340, 2009, pp. 271-461.

Germany) are taken as examples.[8] The hierarchy and interpretation of legal sources, the prevailing way of legal reasoning, the structure of the law, characteristic legal concepts and institutions, and the organization of the judicial system are some of the relevant aspects to reveal the differences and similarities and to explain their existence.[9] If, without any comparisons, merely introductions to the foreign systems are provided, the teaching boils down to the so-called *Auslandsrechtskunde*. Knowing other and different solutions and approaches, however, enables the students to compare.

Another way of teaching comparative aspects of law is to focus on a particular area of law (e.g. corporate or family law), a legal institution (a contract or marriage), or a human right (access to justice) from a comparative perspective, whereby at least two different systems should be included.[10] In a course on comparative tort or property law, for example, the teaching usually includes several other jurisdictions and, specifically in Europe, the European legal order should be one of them. Similarly, in case-oriented comparative law teaching the starting point for the analysis is a case scenario that raises a legal question for research and then guides the students through their work with the legal materials.[11]

Finally, comparative law methodology can be addressed.[12] In this part the first question to be answered is how to define comparative law. It is an academic discipline[13] and it is commonly agreed that a legal comparison is a scholarly process in which specific 'objects' of at least two jurisdictions are set against each other in order (1) to determine their similarities and differences; (2) to explain the causes of the similarities and differences; and (3) to evaluate the solutions.[14] Personally, I think that the methodological part should always be included since only by knowing how to compare will a comparative

---

8   See V. V. Palmer, 'A Descriptive and Comparative Overview', in V. V. Palmer (Ed.), *Mixed Jurisdictions Worldwide: The Third Legal Family*, 2nd ed., Cambridge University Press, 2012, pp. 19–91.

9   Illuminating G. Winterton, 'Comparative Law Teaching', *American Journal of Comparative Law*, Vo. 23, No. 1, 1975, pp. 69-118.

10 See J. M. Smits (Ed.), *Elgar Encyclopedia of Comparative Law*, Edward Elgar, 2006, brings together specific areas of law with introductions to different legal systems and methodological issues.

11 See T. Kadner Graziano, 'A Multilateral and Case-Oriented Approach to the Teaching and Studying of Comparative Law: A Proposal', *European Law Review*, Vol 23, No. 6, 2015, pp. 927-944 (940). This method has been applied by B. Braat, *Indépendance et interdépendance patrimoniales des époux dans le régime matrimonial légal des droits français, néerlandais et suisse*, European Family Law Series, Vol. 6, Intersentia, 2004.

12 See E. Örücü, 'Methodologies for Comparative Law', in J. M. Smits, J. Husa, C. Valcke & M. Narciso (Eds.), *Elgar Encyclopedia of Comparative Law*, Edward Elgar 2023, pp. 42-50.

13 Convincingly argued by C. Valcke, *Comparing Law, Comparative Law as Reconstructions of Collective Commitments*, Cambridge University Press, 2018, pp. 219-223.

14 See K. Boele-Woelki, 'What comparative family law should entail', *Utrecht Law Review*, Vol. 4 No. 2, 2008, pp. 1-24 (7).

law course enable its potential to be developed for the students' later professional career as legal scholars, lawyers or decision makers.[15]

In brief, teaching comparative law entails the challenge of focussing on one or several of the above-mentioned components (the history and the use of comparative law, introductions to other legal systems, teaching a specific legal field from a comparative perspective and comparative methodology) whereby a balance between all four approaches should be achieved.[16] Many books on comparative law[17] provide assistance in reaching the final decision and comparative law teaching in specific areas has also been subject to publications.[18]

---

15 See J. Basedow, 'Comparative Law and its Clients', *American Journal of Comparative Law*, Vol. 62, No. 4, 2014, pp. 821-858.

16 See among others M. Rheinstein, Teaching Comparative Law, *The University of Chicago Law Review*, Vol. 5 No. 4, 1938, pp. 615-625; *Steenhoff*, Teaching Comparative Law, Comparative Law Teaching, Electronic Journal of Comparative Law 2002, https://www.ejcl.org/64/art64-4.html; M. P. Waxman, 'Teaching Comparative Law in the 21st Century: Beyond the Civil/Common Law Dichotomy', *Journal of Legal Education*, Vol. 51, No. 2, 2011, pp. 305-312; J. Husa, 'Comparative Law in Legal Education – Building a Legal Mind for a Transnational World', *The Law Teacher*, Vol. 52, No. 2, 2018, pp. 201-215, F. Cownie, 'Comparative Legal Education,' in: J. M. Smits, J. Husa, C. Valcke & M. Narciso (Eds.), *Elgar Encyclopedia of Comparative Law*, Edward Elgar 2023, pp. 350-357.

17 See M. Siems, *Comparative Law*, Cambridge University Press, 2022; M. Adams & J. Husa & M. Oderkerk, *Comparative Law Methodology: Volumes I & II*, Edward Elgar, 2017; U. Kischel, *Rechtsvergleichung*, C.H. Beck, 2015; M. Adams & D. Heirbauts (Eds.), *The Method and Culture of Comparative Law*, Bloomsbury, 2014.

18 See J. M. Scherpe, 'Comparative Family Law and Family Law Teaching', *in* H. Kha & M. Henaghan (Eds.), *Teaching Family Law, Reflections on Pedagogy and Practice*, Routledge, 2023, Chapter 4; T. Kadner Graziano, *Comparative Contract Law, Exercises in Comparative Methodology*, Edward Elgar, 2023; T. Kadner Graziano, *Comparative Tort Law, Cases, Materials and Exercises*, Routledge, 2018; A. Cahn & D. C. Donald, *Comparative Company Law, Text and Cases on the Laws Governing Corporations in Gemany, the UK and the USA*, Cambridge University Press, 2018.

2 THE ENVIRONMENT OF COMPARATIVE LAW TEACHING

Three aspects determine the environment and consequently the content of comparative law teaching: the expertise of the lecturer, the time available and the target group.[19] The combination of these three aspects is never the same and requires forethought and a flexible approach to the content of the course and the teaching format.

2.1 THE EXPERTISE OF THE LECTURER

The prioritisation of topics will undoubtedly depend on the expertise of the lecturer. What kind of expertise in which areas of law and in which jurisdictions does the lecturer bring to the class? Those who operate in a jurisdiction other than that in which they have received their legal training are predestined to share their comparative experience with students. Knowledge of the main features of some other jurisdictions may also have been gained through comparative research, ideally including a period of study abroad. It will not come as a surprise that talking about one's own comparative research will come naturally. Each and every consideration as to why the comparative legal study was undertaken, under what circumstances, with what aim and purpose, can easily be answered. The similarities and differences between the chosen jurisdictions can be clearly demonstrated and explained, and the final assessment will be convincingly argued. More importantly, the experience of differences in legal cultures and traditions will be more authentically explained. Students feel the commitment and engagement. However, a view on other than one's own comparative approaches and research should likewise be provided.

2.2 AVAILABLE TIME

There are major challenges in terms of the time available. What can students be taught in a 10-14 week course? What should be the focus? For example, the 10-week Comparative Law course at Bucerius Law School in 2023 covered the concept of comparative law and its diverse applications in different fields, the classification of legal systems, how to

---

19 See G. Winterton, 'Comparative Law Teaching', *American Journal of Comparative Law*, Vol. 23, No. 1, 1975, pp. 69-118 (117): "[…] we do not discuss methodology, which depends in the last analysis on the subject-matter taught, the outlook of the students and the inclinaton of the individual teacher."

conduct a comparative legal study, unification and harmonisation, the combination of comparative legal research and interdisciplinarity, and historical comparative research, all with different examples. In contrast, a basic course of only two hours for doctoral students should focus on the method to be used, such as how to conduct a comparative legal study, the difficulties to be overcome, the challenges to be met, and how to present the comparative legal study. A second workshop with such a group of advanced students will provide an opportunity to go into more detail about the topics of the comparative studies they are preparing and to discuss the challenges they face. In such a workshop six questions have to be answered in writing beforehand. This makes it possible to classify the answers, which are then discussed in turn.

1. What is your topic?
2. Which legal systems are you comparing and why?
3. How do you navigate the foreign legal system?
4. How have you structured the presentation and comparison of the legal systems? Simultaneously or successively?
5. Do you combine comparative law with another discipline? How?
6. Do you incorporate findings from other disciplines in your research? How?

In the last few years, more and more attention has been paid to the methodological aspects of a comparative legal study. In 2018, for example, the International Academy of Comparative Law launched a new online journal dedicated to the methodological aspects of comparative law. It covers all fields of law where the methods and techniques of comparative law are at stake. The first topic addressed "The Use of Comparative Law Methodology in International Arbitration", the second topic was on "Comparative Family Law Methodology."[20]

2.3 ADDRESSEES

Finally, the environment in which comparative law is taught is determined by the group of addressees. Who are they? Many different aspects about the students who attend your comparative course should be thoroughly considered before starting, otherwise the mutual expectations will end in disappointment. How much knowledge do they have

---

20 See https://aidc-iacl.org/journal/ (retrieved 30 June 2023). See A. Senegacnik, *Ius Comparatum*, Vol. 1, 2020, Foreword, https://aidc-iacl.org/journal/wp-content/uploads/sites/7/2020/11/IUS-COMPARATUM-VOL-1-1.-A. SENEGACNIK-1.pdf (retrieved 30 June 2023); K. Boele-Woelki, 'Comparative Family Law Methodology: Who, What, Why and How?' *Ius Comparatum*, Vol. 2, 2022, Foreword, https://aidc-iacl.org/journal/wp-content/uploads/sites/7/2022/02/1.-Katharina-Boele-Woelki-Foreword-p.-1-5.pdf (retrieved 30 June 2023).

about their "own" jurisdiction? Are they first, second or third year students or even Master or PhD students? Do they have a specific interest in one of the legal fields, either business law or public law? Have they already gained some experience in comparative law? Have they studied another legal system or have they attended an international summer school?

Most importantly, have they all or the majority of them been educated in the same jurisdiction? Which language skills do they have and is the language in which you are teaching different from the mother tongue of some or all of the students?

By way of illustration I report on the situation at Bucerius Law School where all German students are required to take the English-speaking courses "Introduction to Legal English" and "Foundations of Contract Law" in their first year besides the compulsory subjects in civil, criminal and public law. On a voluntary basis, students can take further courses in other legal languages or general language courses. At the beginning of the third year, everyone is required to study abroad for up to six months at one of our 100 partner universities. The course in comparative law takes place at the end of the third year, so one can build on both some basic knowledge of common law and experiences with other jurisdictions.

In the international programme at Bucerius Law School, which runs from September to December, we welcome 90-100 students from around 25 different countries from our partner universities. They have received their legal education in civil law (e.g. Europe, Asia, South America), common law (e.g. the USA, UK, Australia, New Zealand, Canada) and mixed jurisdictions (e.g. South Africa, Israel). As a result, the programme, which focuses on international and comparative business law, attracts a very heterogeneous group of students. This heterogeneity creates more opportunities to engage students interactively in the classroom. It is this group that has challenged me as to how one can successfully teach the comparative law approach in a short period of time. How can it be effectively done and with lasting effect?

3 METHODS OF COMPARATIVE LAW TEACHING

Comparative law teaching should go beyond simply reading and listening. In class, students expect to engage in undertaking comparisons. The four teaching methods that I have used in my comparative law courses are based on the motto 'learning by doing'. In contrast to a homogenous group of national students, more innovative educational possibilities exist with international students, as they can learn with each other and from each other. Students should learn that there are various solutions to legal problems and that these solutions might either be a source of inspiration to improve one's own law or that they should not be followed. This requires an evaluation based on relevant criteria. How the students internalize this and how they experience looking over the border of their own jurisdiction also depends on the group of students that you want to fascinate in the interesting world of comparative law. Learning by doing turns out to be highly appreciated by the students of a comparative law course. It can be regarded as a stimulus that sets the learning process in motion.[21] Both theoretical knowledge and practical skills are necessary to master a field. Theoretical learning gives the guidance which in turn is converted into practical performance. This cooperation will be demonstrated in the following.

3.1 LEARNING BY EXPLAINING ONE'S OWN LEGAL BACKGROUND

The method of learning by explaining one's own legal background involves the students themselves. They are the main actors. This method is particularly useful and practical for identifying similarities and differences between common law, civil law and mixed jurisdictions. It only works with a heterogeneous group of students from different jurisdictions.

It is up to the lecturer to decide which seating arrangement works best for him or her, but the U-shape is recommended because the students are to be divided into three groups: common law, civil law and mixed jurisdictions. The common law and civil law groups should sit opposite each other, with the students representing the mixed jurisdictions in the middle at the bottom of the U.

---

21 See K. Boele-Woelki, 'Some Reflections on Legal Education: Enriching Critical Thinking Through a Comparative Law Perspective', *in*: M. Linton & M. Sayed (Eds.), *Festskrift till Maarit Jänterä-Jareborg*, Justus Förlag 2022, pp. 23-35.

The lecturer poses specific questions about the main features of the various systems, which are answered by all three groups. Additionally, the students must explain their national system to those who are unfamiliar with it. The students are encouraged to ask clarifying questions about the other systems. The U-shaped layout provides the students with the opportunity to easily see and hear each other. It encourages participation and makes it easy for the moderator to observe students and to intervene when necessary. It creates a sense of equality within the group. The main purpose of the whole exercise is to detect similarities and differences between the various systems. It is a way of bridging the common law – civil law divide. In order to attain this objective, functional questions should be asked by the moderator such as:

1. What sources of law do you use?
2. What type of written law do you distinguish?
3. How does the legislator legislate in your jurisdiction?
4. What are the main legal publications?
5. What are the main features of your system?
6. What role, if any, does the constitution play in your jurisdiction?
7. How do international agreements become binding?
8. What is the role of legal doctrine?
9. Can courts take parliamentary documents into account?
10. How are the courts organised?
11. How does one become a lawyer?
12. How do you become a judge?

It turns out that students are very much engaged in explaining their own system. They sometimes even try to convince the other students that they represent the best system, whereas others take a more critical stance towards their own system. In any case, they listen better if their fellow students explain, if they are asking questions and if they are trying to understand the other system. For some it is a totally strange situation that immediately after law school you can be trained to become a judge, for some a constitutional review of a decision is an alien concept, whereas for others the citing of legal doctrine in decisions or judgments is not possible.

During these discussions, similarities and differences become apparent not only between the common-law and civil-law systems, but also between jurisdictions belonging to the same system. Depending on the topic, it turns out that within the systems to which various jurisdictions belong a great variety of solutions and approaches exist, whereas in turn many similarities between jurisdictions can be discerned which belong to either the civil or the common-law system. A multitude of different aspects can be elaborated which leads to surprises as well as confirmations. Students are creating their own learning-centred environment. The lecture is interrogative, explanatory, reflective and interactive. Students themselves detect the main similarities and differences among the systems. It is their own original experience.

3.2 Comparison on the Basis of the Material Provided

"To think is to compare" is the well-known observation of Walther Rathenau.[22] Both processes can be explained in the context of a legal investigation as follows: While "thinking" is an internal preoccupation that seeks to shape ideas, memories, and concepts into knowledge, "comparing" focuses on contrast; it contrasts the known with the unknown and considers similarities and differences. In English and French, "comparative law" is referred to as comparative law or *droit comparé*. From this, one could infer that comparative law is a field of law rather than a method of finding law. This fallacy, however, would contradict our common understanding of comparative law explained above, whose potential can consequently be used in all areas of law.[23]

When a legal comparison is made, the basic rule of methodology, which has been explicated by Patrick Glenn,[24] becomes immediately relevant. He refers to the linguistic origin of the term 'compare': "Com is from the Latin cum or with and pare is the Latin for equal or peer, so to compare is to exist with another who, though different, is to be treated as an equal." He continues by saying that "Comparison is [...] a process of peaceful coexistence of those who are taken as equals, in spite of even major difference in belief, circumstance or tradition. Comparative lawyers are those who contribute to this process." This explanation reminds us that we should start without any pride and prejudices as far as our 'own' system is concerned when considering whether to compare it with another system, be it a national, regional or international jurisdiction. However, Patrick Glenn's methodological rule does not describe the process of comparative law. This consists of various elements or steps. The description, analysis, explanation and evaluation are to be distinguished. There is agreement that the comparative law process and the requirements to be met follows the definition provided above.[25] Neither vertical nor horizontal comparisons that take place within one and the same

---

22 See W. Rathenau, *Auf dem Fechtboden des Geistes – Aphorismen aus seinen Notizbüchern*, Wiesbaden 1953, p. 32.
23 See E. Örücü, 'Methodological Aspects of Comparative Law', *European Journal of Law Reform*, Vol. 8, No. 1, 2006, pp. 29–42; yM. Van Hoecke, 'Methodology of Comparative Law Research', *Law and Method*, No. 12, 2015, pp. 1–35, retrieved 30 June 2023 from http://www.lawandmethod.nl/tijdschrift/lawandmethod/2015/12/RENM-D-14-00001.pdf.
24 See H. P. Glenn, The National Legal Tradition, Electronic Journal of Comparative Law 2007, retrieved from https://www.ejcl.org/113/article113-1.pdf. See his famous book: H. P. Glenn, *Legal Traditions of the World*, Oxford University Press, 2014.
25 See Chapter 1.

legal system are thus covered by this definition, but only those comparisons that have at least two national, regional or international legal systems as their subject matter.

After introductory explanations on the nature, content, aims and tasks of comparative law, students regularly ask: When do we compare? Comparing rules, institutions, areas of law or principles, however, requires knowledge about the content, objectives and impact of the objects embedded in at least two jurisdictions. As there is no time for students to do preparatory work, a comparative law exercise can also be done in class if the material is selected by the lecturer in advance. Usually, the students are familiar with the legal system in which they have been educated. If it comes to specific areas of law, however, it often transpires that their knowledge only covers the basic features. Very detailed knowledge cannot be expected. In order to enable the students to properly juxtapose various systems, the building blocks for the comparison must be provided. This entails information about the statutory rules and case law of the objects such as, for example, the corporate governance of listed stock corporations or the remedies for a breach of contract by the seller as they are regulated and dealt with in the selected legal systems.

Comparing requires that there *is* something to compare. The comparability of the objects or how *Catherine Valcke* has phrased it "[...] the entities that must exhibit distinctness and adequate interconnectedness if legal comparison is going to be meaningful"[26] is thus decided up front by the lecturer. However, the comparing process and its presentation either orally or in writing does not usually come naturally. It can be practised and, in most cases, it can be improved. Instead of repeating the content of the various answers the comparative material should be presented in a synthesis which combines all components into a connected whole. It consists of grouping, classifying, categorizing, confronting and contrasting the various legal aspects. It can become an art to do it well.

Comparative material that can be used for the comparing process can be easily gathered given the plethora of comparative legal studies.[27] The publications of the topics that are chosen for each World Congress of Comparative Law, for example, consist of a general report, many national reports and a questionnaire.[28] The topics cover all fields

---

26 See C. Valcke, *Comparing Law: Comparative Law as Reconstructions of Collective Commitments*, Cambridge University Press, 2018, pp. 66-67.

27 The compiled publications of all national reports which were drafted as a result of questionnaires by the Commission on European Family Law in the field of divorce, maintenance between former spouses, parental responsibilities, property relations between spouses and informal relationships provide detailed information about family law in Europe. See *European Family Law Series*, Intersentia, Nos. 2, 3, 9, 24, 38.

28 See the *Ius Comparatum – Global Studies in Comparative Law.*

of law. A specific question can be chosen and the answers thereto that are provided by the national reports can be put together in a list containing not more than about five different jurisdictions. The comparative material should entail legal differences. That is why comparisons are mostly undertaken. Beginners in comparative law will often have much more fun finding and explaining differences than coming to the somewhat boring result that things are basically the same in different countries.[29] The students use the comparative material for the comparative exercise. In their presentations, they should classify the various answers. A comparative table in which they can put specific information enables them to dismantle the answers in little bits and pieces.

The answers to the question *Does the surviving partner have rights of inheritance in the case of intestate succession? If yes, how does this right compare to that of a surviving spouse or a registered partner, in a marriage or registered partnership?* given for Austria, Croatia, the Netherlands and Norway, for example, provide information about whether the national systems have legislated on this problem, if not, whether the case law has recognized the inheritance rights of the surviving partner, or whether neither legislation nor judicial decisions have granted such a right. I have provided the students with the following information:[30]

Austria

In contrast to spouses, partners do not have any rights of inheritance. In the case of the death of one partner the surviving partner is neither entitled to inherit, nor does he/she have a right to a compulsory portion (Pflichtteilsanteil). Hence, if a partner wishes to appoint his/ her partner as an heir, it is necessary to draft a last will.

Croatia

In line with Art. 11 paragraph 2 and of the Croatian Family Act and Art. 4 paragraph 2 and Art. 55 of the Croatian Partnership Act, the answer equally relates to both cohabitants and same-sex informal partners. According to Art. 8 paragraph 2 of the Croatian Inheritance Act (Official Gazette no. 48/03, 163/03, 35/05, 127/13) surviving partners in an informal relationship are treated in the same way as surviving spouses if the relationship lasted for a longer period of time and was terminated by the death of one partner, provided that the prerequisites for the validity of a marriage were fulfilled. If these conditions are met,

---

29 See U. Kischel, *Rechtsvergleichung*. Critical Legal Studies, Postmodernism and the Contextual Method in Comparative Law – A Reply to G. Frankenberg, *Zeitschrift für ausländisches öffentliches Recht und Völkerrecht*, 2016, pp. 1009-1016 (1016).

30 These are four out of the twenty-nine answers derived from the national reports that are compiled and structured according to a set of questions *in* K. Boele-Woelki & C. Mol & E. Van Gelder (Eds.), *European Family Law in Action: Informal Relationships*, European Family Law Series, No. 38, Intersentia, 2015, Question 47, pp. 851-864.

the surviving partner becomes an intestate heir, just like a spouse. As an intestate heir, the surviving partner belongs to the first line of succession, together with the deceased's descendants who all equally share the inheritance. If there are no descendants, the surviving partner is placed into the second line of succession, together with the deceased's parents (the parents inherit one half and the partner the other half of the inheritance). If there are no parents, the surviving spouse inherits everything. If the deceased's descendants exist but they renounce their inheritance, the surviving partner is entitled to the entire inheritance.

The Netherlands

In 2003 a completely revised Book 4 of the Dutch Civil Code entered into force, but this did not put formal and informal couples on the same footing. The position of non-marital cohabitants was improved somewhat, but not substantially. No, the surviving partner has no rights of inheritance in the case of intestate succession. According to Art. 4:10 Dutch Civil Code the surviving spouse or registered partner (Art. 4:8 Dutch Civil Code) does have rights of inheritance, but the informal partner does not. The inferior legal position of the surviving informal partner has been criticised in the legal doctrine.

Norway

Surviving cohabitants have rights of inheritance in the case of intestate succession as long as the cohabitants have, have had or expect a child together pursuant to the Norwegian Inheritance Act, S. 28(b). The surviving cohabitant inherits four times the National Insurance basic amount on the date of death – a total of approximately NOK 353,000 or 40,000 Euros. This inheritance right takes precedence over the inheritance rights of the lineal descendants, but can be restricted by a will, as long as the cohabitant is informed of the will before the testator's death. In comparison, the surviving spouse is entitled to one quarter of the estate if the deceased had children and, unlike the right of the cohabitant, this inheritance right can only be partly restricted by a will.

In short, the comparative synthesis reveals the following: Two jurisdictions (Austria and the Netherlands) deny any inheritance rights, whereas in Croatia and Norway the surviving partner has a mandatory right in the case of a qualified partnership (living together for a longer period of time or having common children). In principle, these two jurisdictions belong together; however, a difference exists between both systems. In Croatia, the surviving partner has the same mandatory right as a spouse whereas in Norway this right is limited. The inheritance right is restricted to a certain amount of money and it can also be restricted by a will about which the surviving partner should be informed before the testator's death.

The comparison should detect these nuances and variations. If the legal systems are to be classified into boxes of a table with "yes" and "no" it is important to distinguish between the various levels of similarities ((almost) the same, alike, related, comparable, parallel, analogous, akin) and differences (dissimilar, unlike, unrelated, disparate, contradictory, conflicting, incompatible, irreconcilable). These nuances can only be expressed in writing. When assisting in arranging the details a comparative table is inevitable, but it does not leave sufficient room for subtle differentiations.

3.3 Comparing Comparisons

If we are confronted with the question of "what is comparative law and what is not" – doubts arise about references to foreign law[31] – the canon of generally acknowledged principles regarding the methods for conducting comparative legal studies provide some guidance.[32] In turn, they can be distilled when analyzing comparative studies and this results in *comparing comparisons*. Before explaining what in my view this approach might achieve in legal education, another comparing-comparisons approach should be explained.

A critical stance towards comparative law can also be adopted through an inter-disciplinary approach, i.e. the comparative lawyer can engage with other disciplines which have been founded on the comparative method. This approach has recently been addressed by Geoffrey Samuel.[33] He extensively analyzes comparative literature, comparative history, comparative religions and comparative theology, respectively, as well as the comparison in film studies since they have many useful epistemological and methodological lessons for the comparative lawyer. Not only in these disciplines has the comparative method been employed; comparative economics, comparative sociology and comparative psychology complement the picture.

My comparing-comparisons approach has a different meaning. This approach focuses on the comparison of comparative legal studies and can only be applied if the students have gained some knowledge as to how to undertake a comparative legal study. The aim is to make them aware of the various steps that should be taken, such as which jurisdictions have been chosen and how this has been justified, whether the descriptive parts can be distinguished from the analytical, explanatory and evaluative parts, which sources have been used and what the aim of the comparative study is and whether this has been achieved. The students present specific comparative studies to their fellow

---

31 See G. Samuel, 'Comparing Comparisons', *in* S. Glanert & A. Mercescu & G. Samuel, *Rethinking Comparative Law*, Edward Elgar 2021, p. 160.

32 See S. Besson & L. Heckendorn Urscheler & S. Jubé (Eds.), *Comparing Comparative Law, Publications of the Swiss Institute of Comparative Law*, No. 82, 2017 and H. E. Chodosh, 'Comparing Comparisons: In Search of Methodology', *Iowa Law Review*, 1999, pp. 1027-1131 (1028).

33 See *Samuel*, 'Comparing Comparisons', *in* S. Glanert & A. Mercescu & G. Samuel, *Rethinking Comparative Law*, Edward Elgar 2021, pp. 136-160.

students which have been previously selected. This selection of comparative legal studies in the form of articles, monographs, and – why not? – databases – should represent different formats and cover different fields of law.[34] The students' presentations should emphasize the applied methodology of the different comparative studies. Their theoretical knowledge of the method of comparative legal studies is put into practice. In my experience the students are able to address – without instructing them in advance – at least the following issues when presenting the comparative study.

1. Which jurisdictions were compared?
2. Why were these systems chosen?
3. Who collected the information for each jurisdiction?
4. Does the study include a comparison?
5. Are the differences and similarities explained?
6. Does the author evaluate the different solutions?
7. How is the research presented?
8. How was research from other disciplines (e.g. data) used and integrated into the comparative study?

Such an analytical process includes – depending on the selection of illustrative material – various jurisdictions. It provides insights into the huge variety of comparative legal studies and the different methods of conducting comparative research.[35] A critical scrutiny will prove that the 'quality' of the analyzed comparative research differs. Some of them lack a clear questionnaire or the choice of jurisdictions is not convincing, some lack a consistent comparison whereas others contain national reports which are disjointedly put together. It is up to the students to detect which comparative legal

---

34 In the 2023 Comparative Law Course at Bucerius Law School the students analyzed and presented the following publications: U.S. Library of Congress, Who makes the laws, and how are the laws made? 2016, 2017 and 2018 reports https://tile.loc.gov/storage-services/service/ll/llglrd/2016296553/2016296553.pdf; J. Mair & E. Örücü, *Juxtaposing Legal Systems and the Principles of European Family Law on Parental Responsibilities*, European Family Law Series, No. 27, 2010; G. Williams, 'Same-sex as a human right: How the Strasburg Court could draw inspiration from the US Supreme Court and the Inter-American Court of Human Rights', *Oñati Socio-Legal Series Family Law*, 2023, doi: 10.35295/osls.iisl/0000-0000-0000-1347; M. Pargendler, 'The Role of the State in Contract Law: The Common-Civil Law Divide', *Yale Journal of International Law*, Vol. 43, No. 1, 2018, p. 143; E. Goossens, 'One Trend, a Patchwork of Laws. An Exploration of Why Cohabitation Law is so Different throughout the Western World', *International Journal of Law, Policy and The Family*, Vol. 35, No. 1, 2021, pp. 1–36; Armour *et al.*, 'The Basic Governance Structure: The Interests of Shareholders as a Class', in Kraakman *et al.* (Eds.), *The Anatomy of Corporate Law*, 2017, Oxford University Press, pp. 49–77.

35 See J. Basedow, 'Should Different Types of Methodology in Comparative Legal Research be Combined into one Method?', *Legal Tribune Online*, https://lt.org/publication/should-different-types-methodology-comparative-legal-research-be-combined-one-method (retrieved 30 June 2023). In this video Basedow explains why it is useful to accept the coexistence of different methodologies, which can be applied depending on the examined problem, its background and the goal of its analysis.

study contains flaws and missteps and which take the necessary methodological steps. Usually the students are eager to critically test whether the study fulfils its self-imposed goals and whether – by using the previously provided methodological framework[36] – it can even be classified as a comparative legal study at all. If applicable, they conclude with recommendations to correct any detected flaws.

As a main takeaway it can be noted that analyzing and presenting the comparisons makes the students aware that, for example on the one side, synoptic descriptions of different legal systems can be used as building blocks for a functional comparison and that, on the other, comparative studies provide useful tools (e.g. questionnaires, evaluation criteria) for further research. Most importantly, students learn to read comparative books and articles in a different, more critical way. It makes them think about why a certain step has been taken and whether and how the comparative research can be improved. It brings the comparative method to life, it is critical and reflective.

3.4   UNDERTAKING A COMPARATIVE LEGAL STUDY

The ultimate comparative law experience is to conduct your own comparative legal study. When choosing the object of legal research, there are several reasons to work comparatively. The inclusion of another legal system can question one's own solution, point out alternatives, put existing explanatory approaches into perspective, and provide suggestions for the further development not only of one's own law, but also of foreign law.

The comparative process described here is designed so that all steps are identifiable and presented in a rational manner.[37] A systematic approach is necessary. In particular, the attempt to explain the similarities and differences requires patience and perseverance whereas the evaluation is of great importance for legal policy considerations. The researcher has studied the issue in at least two legal systems and has thus become an expert. The final appraisal is the culmination of a comparative legal study.

If there is good planning of the individual steps in advance, and also if not too many legal systems are involved, conducting a comparative law study is a special research experience. Such a voyage of discovery transcends the boundaries of one's own legal system and creates new knowledge.

---

36   See M. Oderkerk, 'The Need for a Methodological Framework for Comparative Legal Research – Sense and Nonsense of "Methodological Pluralism" in Comparative Law', *RabelsZ*, Vol. 79, No. 3, 2017, pp. 589-623.

37   See K. Boele-Woelki, 'The Working Method of the Commission on European Family Law', *in* K. Boele-Woelki (ed), *Common Core and Better Law in European Family Law*, European Family Law Series No. 10, Intersentia 2005, pp. 14-38.

Choice of jurisdictions

In principle, there are no restrictions in the choice of legal systems, but the goal and subject of the research project as well as personal abilities must be taken into account. The interconnectedness between the research object and the choice of jurisdictions can be illustrated by a few examples: When it comes to the question of whether multi-parenthood should be introduced into German or Dutch law, legal regulatory models for a comparative legal study currently can only be found in England & Wales, British Columbia and Brazil. If it is to be examined whether "nature" should have constitutional rights in environmental law of the European jurisdictions, two countries have already served as models for other legal systems, namely Ecuador and New Zealand. In contrast, when contributing to the design of European private law, the inclusion of several European legal systems is recommended.

It is striking that many comparative legal studies often do not care about small states or entities, their jurisdictions and their laws.[38] They are simply overlooked or not taken seriously. Is it really the size of the territory, population and the gross domestic product (GDP) that matter when selecting jurisdictions for comparative studies? Or are there other reasons for focusing on larger states? They probably provide the most elaborated legal rule or the most effective legal institution; codified laws and/or a wealth of case law is available which has been extensively commented upon by legal scholars or the historical origins of a legal concept can be found there. These are commonly the reasons for selecting a 'significant' jurisdiction when undertaking a comparative legal study. Moreover, the aim of the comparative endeavour might be equally important. If harmonization or unification within a region, such as the European Union, is at stake, all Member States are to be included; however, this does not always happen. The smaller states such as the BENELUX (Belgium, the Netherlands and Luxembourg) are not as often represented in comparative legal studies as Germany, France, Italy, Spain and the United Kingdom. This eurocentrism often also excludes the Scandinavian countries and Eastern Europe. Language barriers might also be blamed for this focus on the centre of Europe since still twenty-three different languages are spoken within the European Union and this will not change in the future. In comparative legal studies in Asia commonly China, Indonesia, Malaysia, Singapore, Thailand and Vietnam are selected, whereas in Africa the divide between Arab, French and English speaking countries are of importance. If it comes to the southern part of Africa, the South African jurisdiction as a mixed jurisdiction as well as due to its modern Constitution and its human rights approach is often taken as a *comparatum* or *comparandum*.

---

38   See T. Angelo & J. Corrin, *Small Sates, A Collection of Essays*, Comparative Law Journal of the Pacific Volume XXIII.

Access to foreign legal systems

The access to foreign sources can be problematic. Not everything is accessible in one's own language or at least in English. At least a passive knowledge of the language spoken in a jurisdiction to be chosen is recommended so that primary sources of law can be used. Translated legal texts are not sufficient for a deeper analysis of foreign law in most cases. Case law and legal literature should be read and analyzed on one's own. If translations are available, it should also be checked how reliable they are. For example, if one uses an English translation of a Bulgarian or Portuguese law, one should be aware of the fact that English is the language of the common law, while the translated law is from a civil law jurisdiction. Common law terminology may have a different meaning in the civil law context. Therefore, it is advisable to consult additional comparative literature in other languages to verify the results.

For comparative legal studies, the Internet is both a blessing and a curse. The Internet makes it possible to quickly gain an overview and find out about the latest changes in the law and about new decisions. Regularly, however, only official websites of governmental and supranational institutions are reliable; many others are not updated and contain outdated or incorrect information. Case law is usually available only in the official language of the jurisdiction selected for the comparative study. If one does not know the specific language, the publications of national experts in other languages in which legislation and case law are analyzed should be consulted. Many recent publications are available electronically, but not all. A visit to well-stocked law libraries is essential.

In particular PhD students should note another preliminary consideration. What are their framework conditions. How much time is available for the comparative legal study? Can more than two legal systems be dealt with, including one's own? What resources (libraries, databases, finances) are available? Depending on the answers to these questions, a stay abroad, possibly several, should be planned and carried out. This should not take place right at the beginning, but only after the researcher has gained a sufficiently good overview in his/her own law and a first orientation in the foreign legal system has taken place. The final collection of material takes place abroad, where the initial insights into foreign law can be examined and discussed with experts from academia and practice. In advance, the admission and supervision possibilities at the respective foreign academic institution must be clarified.

Questionnaire

In order to be able to describe and analyze the object of investigation in the chosen legal systems, the "what" to be compared must be broken down into individual aspects. This is done in the form of questions, all of which are to be answered for the selected legal systems. A functional approach is recommended. The rules and institutions of the different legal systems can only be meaningfully compared if they solve the same factual problem, if they perform the same task and fulfill the same function. This means that the questions are asked in purely functional terms, without reference to the concepts of a particular legal system.

Furthermore, care must be taken that the subject of the investigation, which is, for example, labor law or white-collar crime, is not considered in isolation. Other norms or institutes of the respective legal system must be taken into account. The problem in labor law, for example, may have been influenced by social law and constitutional law, while in white-collar criminal law, corporate law or tax law also play a role. By asking questions, these interrelationships are uncovered.

The questionnaire should contain the most important questions, arranged in a logical order. They can later be used for the headings of the chapters and paragraphs and shortened to the essentials. Thus, they also determine the structure of the comparative law study. The number of questions depends on the subject of the study. The broader the subject, the more questions and vice versa.

For each question, an answer must be given in the respective selected legal systems. Depending on the legal system, codified law and statutes, supreme court rulings and the legal literature explaining them must be used as sources of knowledge. An account focusing only on these is called 'law in the books', while the inclusion of court decisions also from lower courts, sociological or economic studies, interviews with experts, etc. is called 'law in action'. If possible, the latter approach should be used equally. It contributes to a better understanding of the legal solution approach to be discovered.

Comparison

The answers to the questionnaire provide the building blocks for comparison. If the legal systems are only presented as country reports without comparing the approaches to the solution, one speaks of mere *Auslandsrechtskunde*. Although information is provided about one's own and the foreign legal system, they are not compared with each other.

In contrast, the process of comparison consists of identifying similarities and differences. A table in which the answers are entered in abbreviated form is helpful here. This facilitates the overview and the subsequent formulation of the similarities and differences found. It should also be noted that other legal systems should not be viewed solely through the lens of one's own legal system. Not everything that appears to be different at first glance leads to the conclusion, after thorough investigation, that there are in fact different effects and results or that different effects and results are discernible despite (almost) similar formulations.

When identifying similarities and differences, attention must be paid to the so-called *praesumptio similitudinis*. As a rule, the legal systems under study correspond to each other in their results, even if they achieve them in different ways. Two warning functions are attributed to the presumption of similarity. On the one hand, similarities should not be misjudged despite differences; on the other hand, established similarities may ultimately prove to be false. Thus, a thorough investigation is required to make the correct determination.

Finally, superficial quick scans covering many jurisdictions should be avoided. They bear the risk that problems and solutions within the legal culture and system of the respective legal field are not accurately captured and thus may not be correctly related to one's own legal field.

Explanation

Having established the similarities and differences between the legal systems under study, the question arises as to why one legal system has the same or a different solution than the other legal system for the same problem. Consequently, similarities and differences must be explained. Often, not enough thought is given to this important step. The search for explanatory reasons should follow the elaboration of the question and the discussion of the problem under investigation. It also has a clear added value with regard to the final question of which regulation is preferable.

Among the relevant factors, the historical development of the legal systems should be considered first. Are the origins of the subject matter to be found there or is it a regulation that has been received or introduced or amended on the basis of international or regional obligations? The legal materials usually provide the first clues. But social, economic, political, geographical and religious backgrounds may also have influenced convergence or divergence. Finally, the role of jurisprudence may be crucial to change or consistency. The above factors may be equally relevant to similarities as to differences.

Combination of the comparative legal research with other disciplines

Interdisciplinary research has become a solid standing and comparative research is also undertaken in other disciplines. Family relations, for example, are the subject of extensive sociological, pedagogical, psychological, demographic and economic research. Scholars from these disciplines are studying the same real-life events such as partnering, parenting, separation/divorce, blended families and care for children and the elderly. Observing the trend towards more comparative family law, on the one side, and more multi-disciplinary research into family relations, on the other, leads to the question whether, to what extent and how it is possible and necessary to combine comparative legal research with (comparative research in) other disciplines. Of course, this is a question that arises not only in comparative family law, but in all areas of law.[39]

What does this combination entail and which requirements are to be fulfilled? Exploring some methodological aspects of combined comparative research requires to distinghuish between basically two approaches: If the combined comparative research consists of comparative legal research which includes at least two legal systems and research into the same problem from another or various other disciplines which is conducted in the very same countries that have been selected for the comparative legal study we can indicate such an approach as *synchronized comparative research*. If combined comparative research consists of comparative legal research which includes at least two legal systems and research into the same problem from another or various other disciplines conducted in one of the countries that have been selected for the comparative legal study or that has been undertaken in other countries the term *restricted comparative research* is appropriate.[40]

Evaluation

The critical evaluation of solutions is an essential part of comparative legal research. It must be borne in mind that the legal institutions and norms of a legal system and their application in legal practice are an expression of a system of values, and that the relevant values – and in particular their weighting – vary from one legal system to another. There is no globally recognized canon of values with a uniform hierarchy, which is why there are no truly objective standards for evaluation; therefore, a certain degree of subjectivity

---

39   See A. S.-M. van Aaken, 'Vom Nutzen der ökonomischen Theorie des Rechts für die Rechtsvergleichung', *in* Jahrbuch junger Zivilrechtswissenschaftler 2000, Richard Boorberg Verlag 2001, pp. 127-141.
40   See K. Boele-Woelki, 'Combined comparative research in the field of family relations: Some reflections from the legal perspective', *Special Issue Journal of Family Research/Zeitschrift für Familienforschung* 2015, pp. 238-256.

inevitably remains. If the critical evaluation of the solutions to the substantive problem identified in the individual legal systems is carried out on the basis of named criteria, this will do justice to the necessary balance. What matters here is the choice of evaluation criteria. These may, when properly examined, direct one or another solution as preferable. Depending on the object of investigation, the following criteria are useful as a basis for evaluation: safety and ease of traffic, protection of the status quo/confidence, legal certainty, protection of the weaker party, the welfare of the child, transaction costs, efficiency, etc.

The assessment or evaluation forms the final part of the comparative legal study. Here, the personal opinion of the researcher is called for. This can give recommendations for improving one's own law, but also conclude that one's own law meets the evaluation criteria, while there is a need for reform in the other legal systems. However, any criticism, especially of foreign legal systems, should be formulated cautiously, because law is socially and culturally shaped. It is a consequence of a historical development and the economic and religious circumstances found in explaining the similarities and differences found should be respected. Accordingly, the manner and justification of how proposals for improvement are formulated determine the degree of persuasiveness.

Presentation of the comparative research

The presentation of the comparative research requires a few specific considerations. In the introduction, after discussing the research question, the selection of the legal systems studied must be justified. Here, the considerations made in the preliminary phase come into play. Furthermore, it must be decided and, if necessary, discussed whether a successive or simultaneous presentation of the legal comparison is to be made. In the case of the successive method, individual country reports are prepared, each of which deals with all aspects of the legal system presented in turn, while in the case of the simultaneous method, the presentation is divided into sub-questions, within the framework of which the legal system examined in each case is explained.

There is no general preference for one or the other method of presentation. Whether the comparative legal study proceeds successively or simultaneously depends on the number of questions, but also on personal preference and feasibility. In both options, the same questions are asked and answered. In the simultaneous presentation, more emphasis is placed on the comparison, which takes place directly after the presentation of the individual sub-aspects of the object of study, whereas in the successive presentation, the comparison takes place only at the end. It requires a good memory with regard to the previous presentations, which can cover quite a large scope for many questions. Furthermore, the time element must also be taken into account. The selected legal systems are not examined at the same time, but usually one after the other. Therefore, the collection of material is often done first in the form of country reports. A second processing, which then includes the comparison, can be done simultaneously if the focus is to be directed to the partial questions. A combination of both modes of presentation is also possible. It should only be done if a logical distinction can be made in, for example, substantive law on the one hand and international private law references on the other.

As a result issues like how to frame a research question (functional or institutional), the selection of jurisdictions, how to split a legal problem into part problems and how to draft a questionnaire, which and how sources (the Internet, handbooks, statutory rules, legal journals) should be used, how to structure the report (simultaneous or successive comparison) et cetera need to be addressed before the students can get started. For the supervision of such a comparative experience, sufficient preparatory and instruction time is needed.[41] Undoubtedly, however, conducting research into at least two jurisdictions by oneself and writing a comparative paper provides the students (usually a team of two or three) with valuable insights into the challenges of becoming a comparatist. At least that is my experience from my Utrecht days, where we evaluated student performance based on such a research and writing experience.[42] In this exercise, the students themselves are the main actors. How they deal with the comparative material, how they process it and, above all, how they present it, should be supervised and finally graded. Such an exercise belongs at the Master's or doctoral level. There, the methodological considerations of why, what and how are important and should be addressed before the comparative research has started. Often, however, due to the limited time for a comparative law course, a student assignment of undertaking a comparative legal study is not manageable.

---

41   See S. Koch, 'From Mapping to Navigation – a COMPASS Formula for Conducting Comparative Analysis', *in* S. Koch & J. Øyrehagen Sunde (Eds.), *Comparing Legal Cultures*, Fagbokforlaget 2020, pp. 71-103.

42   The assessment of the comparative papers can be based on the following grounds: *Structure*: Logical division of topics into different sections; *Analysis* of different opinions in legislation, case law and legal literuatre; *References*: Use of recent literature and relevant details and correct citations; *Comparative synthesis*: a clear presentation of similarities and differences and the attempt to explain them; *Evaluation*: the arguments used to support one's own opinion.

4   FINAL RECOMMENDATIONS

In a legal methodology course, students want to reflect and discuss. Particularly a comparative law course facilitates critical thinking by looking beyond one's own jurisdiction,[43] as familiar solutions are challenged and contrasted. Students want to experience this for themselves because their own experiences and reflections are both not only exciting but also the most memorable for them. However, as comparative law also requires a good knowledge of other legal systems, but the time available in a course is short, some practical help is needed to make the experience of comparative law enjoyable in the long term.

Finally, I would like to recommend that a comparative law course should seek to achieve three objectives: curiosity and openness to the other, the unknown; an understanding of the different methods of comparative law; and a reflection on the steps required in a comparative legal study – when and why to take which step.

---

43   See K. Boele-Woelki, 'Some Reflections on Legal Education: Enriching Critical Thinking Through a Comparative Law Perspective', *in* M. Linton & M. Sayed (Eds.), *Festskrift till Maarit Jänterä-Jareborg*, Iustus Förlag, 2022, pp. 23-35.